T0352988

# Kingfisher

ENCOUNTERS IN THE WILD

JIM CRUMLEY

*Saraband*

# ONE

A SMALL, BROWN BIRD is flying towards me where I sit on a riverbank; brown but with a tiny, curved triangle of bright white at its throat, like a neatly folded cravat. It flies downstream a little above head height, and its flight is fast and dead straight.

I know what you are thinking:

"A small, brown bird – can't you be a bit more specific, you being a nature writer?"

To which the answer is yes and no. I can sense your disappointment.

But I am having a problem with this particular brown bird. Two problems, if I am being honest. Firstly, it is *very* small. Not wren-small, but in the context of hundreds of yards of tree-shrouded river, small enough for me to think I did well to

1

spot it in the first place. Secondly, because it is flying head-on and ever-so-slightly higher than my line of sight, and because it won't deviate, won't bank one way or the other, won't leave the deepest shadow of the trees, all I can see is its head-on head, breast and underwings, and all these (forby the jaunty cravat), are brown, and, in that particular tree-shaded absence of light, dull brown.

And now that it occurs to me, there is a further consideration. Not troublesome enough to constitute a third problem, perhaps, but a mitigating consideration nevertheless, and it is this: I know this stretch of river well – I sit here often and I walk here as often as I sit here – and I know what to expect on a regular basis and what is likely to turn up from time to time. That does not mean that I am never surprised, far from it, but here – and much more often than not – I rejoice in the familiar. The suddenly revealed tricks of light and weather (a restless, ever-present pageant along Scotland's Highland Edge, perched precariously between Highlands and Lowlands), or the interaction between, say, otter and beaver, or redstart and grey wagtail, or osprey and red kite, or hundreds of martins and swallows that take time out from hunting to cluster angrily round a golden eagle just down from the mountains on a casual hunting foray of its own…all that amounts to variations on known and well-loved themes.

But then one day, I walk where I usually walk, I sit where I usually sit (a bend in the river with good views up and downstream, and where a small burn eases through a breach in the river-bank and enlivens both the texture and the music of the mainstream), and suddenly I am scratching my head at the imminent arrival of a small, brown bird. Three or four seconds more and all will be revealed, but I am still head-scratching. So when I reply "yes and no" to your question about specifics, it is only because the way the bird is flying and where it is flying suggests one thing to me, but the brown-ness suggests that perhaps I am wrong.

Then at fifty yards and closing, the bird speaks. It does so in a thin, high-pitched and far-carrying voice, and the voice tells me at once that I was right all along, and the brown-ness was a fluke of sightlines.

"*Cheeeek!*" it says, then: "*Cheeeekee!*"

Then it whizzes past me and bursts into flames.

Blue flames, searing shades of blue, the most startling, the most strident, the most breathlessly beautiful BLUE. And all the while I had thought it was brown. The change of angle from head-on to side-on, and then the rear view, reveals the king-fisher in all its considerable array of glories, and for good measure it burns straight through a patch of downstream sunlight and leaves a streak of blue dazzle on the air there, like diamond dust.

But who would have thought that a kingfisher could ever just be brown? I have seen kingfishers often enough over about forty years, but this is the first time I have been compelled to consider that it is possible to see one and – in certain circum-stances – dismiss it as a small, brown bird. So I have just made a promise to myself that I will try not to let that happen again.

◉ ◉ ◉

Colour is to kingfishers what slipperiness is to eels. The particular quality of their plumage that startles, that makes gibberish-peddlers out of field guide compilers and induces frustrated poets to throw themselves from tall cliffs, is nothing more than an ingenious arrangement of shades of blue, all but one of which are unexceptional in their own right, but which are downright sensational when they are so intricately and inspirationally juxtaposed with each other and with solid patches of smoky orange (not brown at all, not when you see them in good light!).

The one rare shade of blue is an irregular streak of pale, sunlight-on-Hebridean-summer-sea kind of blue that extends the length of its neck, back and tail. But it also recurs sporadically like exotic freckles on the top of the bird's head and on its eyebrows (where it mottles two further background shades of darker blue), on narrow stripes along the cheeks, and to spectacular effect as spots, stripes and tapering patches on the top of its wide-open wings. If there is anything more flamboyantly *haute couture* in all the fauna of the land, I have not seen it.

But there's more.

In the right kind of light, the primary wing feathers alternate a muted shade of that extraordinary blue with deeply-toned lilac. Then there is the orange: a cheek triangle (this gives way to a worn-backwards dog collar of bright white extending round the back of the neck), and deeper and darker orange flanks and belly and part of the underwings. The final embellishments are scarlet legs and feet, and (tucked away with what little discretion a kingfisher can muster) that little glimpse of white cravat. Oh, and the whole thing is set off with a black and red dagger of a bill as long as its head.

I cannot help wondering what evolution was up to when it went to such trouble to make kingfishers stand out from the crowd, and all this for a bird that would be the same size as a sparrow were it not for that fish-snaring bill. There is a widespread belief that the effect is designed to warn would-be predators that kingfisher flesh tastes disgusting, but I detect a hint of the mediaeval at work in that particular theory, which in turn makes me wonder if Shakespeare wrote it somewhere, just as he invented and gave universal credibility to the idea that swans sing as they die (they don't!). It is still regurgitated endlessly as a kind of ornithological mantra, although I have yet to meet anyone who can identify the source, or who is prepared to admit that they have first-hand experience of what a kingfisher tastes like. There are other wild birds out there that cut a dash but don't come with a health warning – green woodpeckers, yellow-hammers, black grouse, redstarts, yellow wagtails and bullfinches, for example. Why would the idea adhere only to kingfishers?

There is a singularly memorable little TV film replaying in my head. It was about a river, and what made it memorable for me was a sequence in which two female kingfishers were locked in what was quite literally mortal combat. The fight eventually collapsed onto the surface of the water, at which point the two birds hurtled downstream at the speed of the current. Yet neither of them would loosen its grip on the other and it looked as if the only outcome would be that one of the birds – or both of them – would drown. The decisive intervention came from a mink that had laid an ambush, timed its attack perfectly, and disappeared into the undergrowth of the bank with one of the kingfishers in its mouth. Almost at once it returned in pursuit of the second kingfisher (so now we know that mink can count up to two at least), but the bird had recovered its wits sufficiently to fly up to a bankside branch where it perched, looking as drab and bedraggled and colourless as a Victorian kingfisher that had been stuffed and mounted in a glass case in a sunlit window for about 150 years.

Adding insult to what must have been quite a repertoire of injuries, her mate suddenly appeared, as pristine and gleaming as a kingfisher by Fabergé, pounced onto her back, mated with her where she stood, then vanished, leaving her alone again to ponder the sequence of events that had just befallen her.

In turn, I am left to consider that (a) the mink hasn't read the health warnings about kingfisher flesh, (b) it has, but doesn't care what the flesh tastes like as long as it's flesh, or (c) it's colour-blind, in which case the kingfisher's flashy plumage is completely useless, and it may as well have been just another little, brown bird.

# TWO

IT'S WET.

By "it", I mean everything.

The entire world as I know it is wet.

The air is wet. The rusty, old gate is wet, so wet that it will be rustier than ever by tomorrow. The ankle-deep grass is wet. The oak trees are wet. Even the patches of relative shelter under the oak canopies are wet, because every now and then a breeze ruffles the leaves and wherever raindrops have gathered into tree-drops among the clustered oak leaves, they spill water in fat wedges.

The little burn that flows slow and dark-green-shadowed through dense and untrampled woodland for the entirety of its brief existence is a demented drumskin on which the hissing paradiddle of falling raindrops and tree-drops makes merry. The burn ends at the bend in the river.

# KINGFISHER

There it sees the sky for the first time, and sunlight on the right kind of day, but this is not one of those. A weeping willow of fifty summers and five trunks leans out from the far bank towards the burn's whimpering, whispering arrival. The willow is wet, actually weeping. It dispenses a constant shower of rainwater from the trailing ends of its down-curving branches. The first hints of imminent autumn have rather crept up on it, and its foliage has begun to pale and thin, which has the effect of speeding up the run-off of rainwater in a wide semi-circle. The result is a flimsy curtain of water drops, the frailest and the most exquisite waterfall you ever saw.

The mountain is wet. The little I can see of it (about the bottom third) reveals a ribbon of white froth where no water was falling at all this time last week. The entire land is agitated with the overwhelming restlessness of water on the move, and for the moment I feel like the still centre amid so much wet chaos.

I am wearing head-to-toe waterproofs and wellies, and I am sitting on the riverbank on a very small, lightweight, collapsible, aluminium-and-fabric tripod stool. Half an hour ago, a very wet kingfisher blurred past me going upstream and vanished round the bend in the river.

Why am I still here?

Because I have been waiting ever since, in the hope that it might come back. This is one of those situations which is much more interesting on the inside than it sounds from the outside.

I don't mind being wet. I'm a Scottish nature writer working in Scotland. It rather comes with the territory. And I like bends in rivers. I like the perpetual anticipation of the unexpected. The kingfisher could be back at any moment. It took me by surprise the last time because I was looking upstream and it arrived from behind me so I only saw the back view. I wouldn't want to miss the moment when it returns. Over half an hour more, the rain eases to a smirr, the sky lightens, the mountain shrugs off all but a skullcap of rain cloud. A dipper has followed the identical midstream flightpath of the kingfisher, and it hasn't come back either.

A heron rises from behind the willow, sees me, exhales a breathy rasp of disapproval, and ducks back down behind the tree. I have been passing time by trying to draw the willow. It's not going too well. I was never taught to draw, willows or anything else, and it shows. I wonder about incorporating the heron into the drawing but I lack the courage, that and the ability to draw herons. Besides, drawing should be an end in itself, not a displacement activity. What I hope is that the kingfisher comes back around the bend on the inside line and perches in the lowest branch of the willow. Then I can include it in the drawing as an impressionistic smudge with a chunky, tapering beak. Even I can probably manage that.

A lot of the art of nature writing is waiting for something to turn up. You cannot force the pace. I believe there is no substitute for the kind of stillness that permits you to become part of the landscape, so that many of nature's tribes treat you as if you don't exist, or better still that you do exist but as an accepted part of the landscape. Mostly, that's when nature confides in you, not knowing you are there, or knowing you are there but deciding it can afford to take a chance on your presence. On the other hand, there are days like this, when the kingfisher doesn't turn up again, and nothing else does either.

So I watch the river. I watch the light grow brighter in two furrows out in midstream, I watch the patterns of water in the shadow of the willow, I lean closer to the land.

One of my favourite Scottish singers, Dougie MacLean, wrote in one of his songs: *It's the land, you cannot own the land, the land owns you.*

It takes a day like this to understand finally what he meant.

⊛ ⊛ ⊛

On more tranquil days, the little burn arrives at the bend in the river more demurely, leaving behind it a life lived in bottle green tree shadows. With an audible sigh that sounds like gratitude, it ripples into a languorous mainstream curve of sun-glitter. And that weeping weeping willow leans out from the opposite bank almost as far as midstream, shaping an elegant arch of a shade of green so pale you could almost say it was white. The profound tranquillity conferred on that meeting of waters by the willow arch is sundered at irregular, unpredictable intervals by the searing passage of kingfishers. It is a place that has grown on me in a few short years, but it was not the kingfishers that lured me here originally.

There is a second willow on the riverbank, smaller and much more inconspicuous than its neighbour. If you sit here, looking across the water to the willows, your eye may eventually be caught by an unusual growth of tall, dense, deep-green foliage, apparently emerging straight from the water and a yard out from the bank where the smaller willow stands. It is an exceptional illusion, or at least it is in this part of the world. Flag irises and marsh marigolds flourish there amid reedy grasses, but what you cannot see now, with the river this high, is the nature of their seedbed. When I first stopped at this exact spot, it was because I had stumbled on a sight that had been missing from the waterways of Scotland for the better part of 400 years. It was a low wall made of what must have been hundreds of sticks, a few stones, and a great deal of riverbed mud to bind the whole edifice together. It was about twenty feet long, between two and three feet high, and it sloped gently down from a flattened top a yard wide. It was a beaver dam. So it was not kingfishers that lured me to this bend in the river but beavers.

I had become aware of the relationship between beavers and kingfishers about a year earlier, while researching my book about beaver reintroduction in Scotland, *Nature's Architect* (Saraband, 2015). On the River Earn, about a dozen miles north-east of this Trossachs backwater, beavers had excavated a short canal, creating a channel of quiet water and a dammed pool just yards from the often boisterous main river, and parallel to it. Not only did the canal provide a perfect sanctuary for small fish, and the pool a nursery water for the young of bigger fish, it was an immediate hit with

the local dippers and kingfishers. They were in
there exploring its possibilities before the digging
was finished, before the pool was dammed and
deepened.

Such is the nature of beavers. They manipu-
late land and water to their own ends, and in the
process they enhance life's possibilities for innu-
merable fellow travellers, like kingfishers.

So now, sitting on the bank by the bend in this
Trossachs river, and a dozen miles to the south-
west of that canal-and-pool complex, and four
years after I first came face to face with the beaver
dam by the small willow, the dam has done what
beaver architecture does after the beavers move
on, which is to break down, evolve at nature's
bidding, and reinvent itself. The American poet
Robert Frost called it "the slow, smokeless burning
of decay". In the midst of a wet summer with the
river consistently high, you cannot see a single
stick, just a long, thin strip of water garden.

I am as sure as I can be that this dam was the
work of a single beaver looking for either a new
territory, or for other beavers, or for both. They

are not yet well established in the river system of the upper Forth, but there have been quite a few explorers who have come over the hill from their stronghold in the Tay river system, of which the Earn is a component part.

# THREE

FINALLY, THIS LESS THAN SUMMERY SUMMER has contrived a perfect morning. Ben Ledi, the mountain that heaves across the northern skyline, seems to have sprawled a little more, and greened then yellowed a little in a ripening way, and that shade is embellished by the slow passage of cloud shadows across its highest slopes, an extraordinary blue-black species of beauty.

No sooner have I reached the riverbank than a heron lifts from a river-watching stance in a fold in the ground, floats vertically over the trees, puppet legs dangling loosely, and vanishes. No matter how carefully, how softly I arrive, it never seems to be careful enough or soft enough to outwit the herons. The river seems unusually quiet, respectful of the morning. Its voice offers nothing more than the burn's perpetual sigh and an added layer of murmur where it rustles over a small promontory of stones. A sedge warbler calls from the reedy grass beyond the far bank, unseen, as sedge warblers usually are. The voice is thin, harsh, comical, repetitive, and subscribes to no known definition of the word "warble". An hour passes in which nothing else moves or calls. A species of agreeable-enough torpor sets in, but it is a state of mind that is not conducive to good nature writing.

Then: *fizz*!

The kingfisher tears upstream, ruffles the very air not a yard above the surface and startles the eyes (every time, no matter how often, the eyes startle and never accustom themselves to what passes). It is *the* brightest blue, brighter than my last memory of it, brighter than where my imagination has pitched it in its absence, even in the darkest river-tree shadows to which its flight clings. Then, at the moment it banks right to follow the bend in the river, it crosses a small square of sunlight, and *that* shade of blue flares with an icicle sheen.

Then gone.

Two seconds?

Three, at a push.

But the morning, the river, the willows, the watcher on the bank…all are enlivened, enriched, renewed. What other bird does that? In two seconds?

Another hour tiptoes by, another hour of burn sigh, river murmur. Clouds begin to fleck the sky as they so often do on crystal summer noontides. A silken calm descends. The kingfisher must come back, so sit still, wait, become riverbank. Then on the stroke of noon, the day stirs. Nature rouses, exhales, a warm breeze animates the willows, the grass, the reeds, the waterworld plants of the old beaver dam. The oaks behind me, less prone than willows to a stirring breeze, contrive a kind of shrug. Birds mobilise: the fallen-silent sedge warbler resumes, a song thrush crosses the river and perches in an oak. No song though. A dipper arrives, lands among the stones where the river mutters, and not five yards away, then wades chest-deep where the water covers a small shingle bed, feeding the lazy way (for a dipper) without diving down to walk on the riverbed. Drops of water gleam on its feathers (biologically, it's a large, waterproof wren), and when it perches it throws something between a shadow and a reflection on the water, the image animated by rippling water. Nature as surrealist painter.

But where are the kingfishers? The bend in the river reveals no sudden blue flashlight, no burnt orange offering, no head-on brown bird, for all that I stare at it for minutes at a time and with and without binoculars, and in between bites of a riverbank lunch. Finally, after who knows how long, a certain weariness creeps in. I recognise its symptoms, and it is my own way of telling myself that time's up, for the quality of the watching is impaired. One last resigned sweep of the glasses then, back along the riverbank, but in my mind I'm already heading for the nearest café. That sweep pauses at the base of the big willow where the five trunks meet their reflections, and the king-fisher is there, perched on the outermost end of the lowest, thinnest branch, upright as a garden gnome. How the hell did it get there?

# KINGFISHER

It flies a few yards to the next willow, the spindly one with the old beaver dam for company. When I first laid eyes on the dam, the beaver had already moved on. Around the same time, one was filmed not far away by some canoeists, then there were no more sightings. But the dam was still intact, and it was clear that its purpose was to create an area of calm water by the bank, and quite possibly it protected a burrowed underwater entrance into a temporary lodge in the bank. And although the dam is now nothing like as clearly defined, it still achieves its original purpose, and that quiet, shallow pool between dam and bank is as alluring as ever for the neighbourhood kingfishers.

This one perches in the willow's lowest branch, although it's still four feet above the surface, unlike the five-trunked willow with its trailing fringes dipping in and out of the water. The bird is side-on, the perfect profile, fifty-fifty blue and orange. And as it shuffles two or three sideways steps towards the end of the branch, there are glimpses of outrageously scarlet feet. Then it dives.

The dive is executed behind the beaver dam,

so only the launch is visible, although there is an audible splash. Four or five seconds elapse between the dive and the reappearance on the same perch, but this time facing the other way, and with a two-inch-long fish a-twitch in its bill. Half a dozen violent thumps of the fish head against the branch take care of the twitches, then the fish is gone, head first. It is hard to suppress a grin. There is something perversely comical about such a stylish creature deploying such brutal technique. This is not a wolf bringing down a deer, or a peregrine falcon plucking a racing pigeon from the air, this is slapstick. Although it is fair to say that the fish would have an alternative point of view.

A simple equation presents itself. More beavers equals more young fish in quiet, shallow waters, which equals more kingfishers.

⊛　⊛　⊛

Twelve days later, and in my absence the flood-plain beyond the willows' bank is candy-flossed with meadowsweet, and the bank where I like to sit has acquired bluebells. These are not the widely mis-named bluebells of springtime's bluebell woods (which are more properly wild hyacinths) but the Scottish bluebell that the English language insists is a harebell. The Latin name is *Campanula*, which means a small bell, and it is demonstrably a blue bell, and hares have nothing to do with it. The flower, of course, doesn't care much what we call it. There is no more lovely ornament to the summer riverbank, and I am an unashamed fan.

For once, the river is stunned by sunlight and heat. I move from my accustomed seat to the shade of some oak trees very close to where the burn emerges. From here the view changes, and includes the next bend a hundred yards upstream. I suspect the bank on the outside of that second bend might accommodate the nest (it looks suitable at this distance), but the terrain between here and there is inaccessible without (a) a canoe, and (b) knowledge of how to propel one expertly through variable river currents, and I possess neither. With the dilemma still unresolved in my mind, a kingfisher hurtles past me and into the upstream straight, but where it would have to deviate if it was heading towards the suspected nest site, it takes the second bend flat out on the racing line and vanishes, leaving the shattered remnants of my theory in its wake. Vanishing and theory-shattering are what kingfishers do best.

I want to know what happens next, how to compose a sounder theory. But the riverbank becomes un-navigable here, grows jungly, and fankles progress with fallen trees and waist-deep channels that dart away from the mainstream then rejoin further down, carving the land into densely wooded and overgrown little islands. Yet within these luxuriantly treed backwaters either side of the mainstream lie quiet pools overarched by slim tree trunks and slimmer limbs, and if only I can find a way in, I suspect I might find there a kind of kingfisher underworld. It proves to be much easier than I had imagined.

A single-track road burrows between high and dense summer hedges, and more or less follows the river's course upstream, but at a discreet and unseen distance. I follow it for a while, looking for a weakness, a way in. And there it is, a rusted gate immobilised by age and overgrown with vegetation but easily climbable, and after a few jungly yards on the other side there is a narrow, mown path through the waist-high undergrowth. It leads back downstream, following one of those backwaters of the main river from beginning to end, separated from the bank only by an unbroken verge of trees and shrubs and grass and reeds; unbroken, that is, except that here and there the mower has smoothed a breach through the verge to the water's edge.

The only problem is sightlines. There aren't any. Back at my habitual post by the bend in the river, there is a view of 150 yards of downstream river and fifty upstream, and by moving to the shade where the burn enters, there is a further stretch of 100 upstream yards before the second bend. Mostly, of course, the kingfishers navigate it at speed. But the idea of a kingfisher underworld somewhere along this mown path has taken hold. My pace slows, my progress is silent; anticipation evolves into a sense of imminent destination.

Finally, the backwater slithers through its deepest, darkest stretch then eases in silence back into the mainstream. At once, the bankside vegetation is gone, and instead, the unknown mower has cleared a wide swathe to the riverbank. The river itself curves out of a long straight into a kind of wide basin, where the current slows as it negotiates shingle banks and gravel banks, deep pools and fallen trees. The place is hidden from every direction, and sunlight pours in. Trees crowd down to the far bank. And on the downstream exit from the basin, just as the current quickens again, there is another small and densely treed island. Trees soon crowd in again on my side of the basin and the mown path narrows again and creeps to a hidden cul-de-sac where a thin screen of willow branches is open enough to permit a watcher another 100 downstream yards. It is through that screen that a kingfisher appears, calling, and disappears round the far side of the island. Almost at once an unseen but much closer bird responds. I have found my underworld.

There is a second response behind the island

and a glimpse through the trees of a flying king-fisher. Seconds later, it speeds out into the main-stream round the near end of the island, fashions a tight right turn into the basin and the blaze of sunlight, and there it too catches fire. It passes by no more than ten yards out from the bank, cutting a diagonal across the water before another right turn takes it back into tree shadows where its fiery plumage cools, and seconds later it has vanished upstream.

Damn.

An undercurrent of frustration attends these fast fly-pasts, and somehow the level twitches up a step or two if it involves the off-on-off sorcery of a flight from shadow to sunlight and back to shadow. What I need – what I think the kingfisher under-world might bring to the table – is the changed behaviour of the birds at their destination. No sooner has the thought lodged than a new king-fisher voice sounds, improbably close.

Turn towards the sound. But resist the urge to move quickly. Turn slowly. This time the bird is not hard to find. It's thirty yards away on a midstream perch where a river-borne tree limb with attendant branches has snagged against a low branch of an alder on the downstream edge of the island, and become anchored there. The kingfisher's perch is four feet above the water. It faces me, stares straight at me. The composition is mostly full-on orange with blue edging and trim white cravat.

It looks like this year's model, the fully fledged progeny of an early brood, with all the colours in place but none of the dazzle. If this had been my first kingfisher, I might have wondered what all the fuss was about. Instead, I return the level gaze, try a one-sided mental experiment, seeking out its wavelength. It goes something like this:

*How long have you been there?*

*And have you been watching me all that time?*

*I know it's no more than a minute, but by the standards of my track record here, which is all fast passing glances, a minute of kingfisher scrutiny is something of a marathon.*

*Do you perch there to fish?*

*Unlikely. That's dipper's fishing terrain below you, not kingfisher's.*

# KINGFISHER

*The water below your branch gathers in a chattering rush just out from where the island tapers like the bow of a boat, mainstream to starboard and the backwater from the far side of the island to port, and the two currents fusing just a yard downstream of your perch, all ripples and riffles, all surge and bustle.*

That seems to be too complex a thought, for the kingfisher shudders, re-orders its plumage, takes off, U-turns in not much more than its own length, dives under the branch where it perched a moment ago, tears off downstream a few inches above the water. Just when I thought I was getting somewhere, too.

# FOUR

A LIVELY SUMMER DAY gathers rain-darkened clouds among piles of white cumulus and sudden blue sunlight, and hefty breezes gather momentum when showers hiss over the river and throb through the trees. All is movement and restlessness, not least the light. Shadows and sunlight chase each other downstream and across the highest mountain slopes. The woods, the river, the burn, the birds, are fidgety and gossipy. The mood is infectious.

There is a young heron on the path, twenty yards away. For once, I have seen it first. It stands side-on to me, and looks like a loosely furled grey umbrella (its beak is the handle) that someone has stuck in the ground and forgotten about. I congratulate myself on outwitting it with my stealth, but crucially, I have missed the second and third herons, for they are standing in the water and hidden by reeds and shrubs and trees. But they see me, or somehow sense me. They fly first, and they also spook the umbrella into unfurling flight.

The first kingfisher flies by the island there, low and fast downstream. A second follows five minutes later. Then for one and a half hours there is nothing at all. Such is the erratic tempo of kingfisher watching, unless you stake out a nest at nesting season, but that is not my preferred way of working. Then both reappear together but in their head-on, brown-bird guise, and I have started to recognise that now, to know what it looks like without guessing. I have also noticed that when they fly downstream, they pass the island on the right, and when they fly upstream, they go round the narrow "blind side" of the island, and sometimes they emerge from that side and sometimes they don't.

This time, they both emerge, side by side and a yard apart and a yard above the water. They follow the bends in the river and vanish. I decide to follow upstream, at least as far as the quieter pool, retracing my steps of two hours ago. There is a gap a few inches wide between two alders, and through it I can see that the riverbank beyond has new occupants – a female goosander and eight chicks. They are all sitting on a patch of short grass, and all facing the water. Not one bird moves. The discipline of a brood of goosanders is something to behold.

The adult bird sits off to one side of the brood, looking straight ahead, keeping dead still. The chicks imitate her pose, sit in two parallel rows of three, one row behind the other, and two more sit side by side a yard from the front rank of three. They are half-sized versions of their mother, and all wear the same team colours: chestnut brown head with rakish, punkish headdress; breast a handsome shade of Burgundy wine; soft grey back; white flanks. Were it not for the haircut, they would be positively demure.

It is their rigid immobility that fascinates. They are clearly taking a break from fishing, but they look taut, more tense than resting, primed to hit the water at the first hint of trouble. Trouble, as it turns out, comes in the shape of the watcher. As

I ease myself into a slightly better position for a slightly better view, a misplaced foot finds itself up to the ankle in water and temporarily unbalances its owner. The noise is not loud, but it is unnatural and it is enough.

The female leads with an explosive run from a sitting start and a curving dive into the river. The chicks simply follow suit, but instead of mass panic they go in single file, each one waiting its turn as if the thing had been choreographed in a hundred rehearsals. I like to think that evolution knew what it was doing when it came up with this technique, but if the intruder had been, say, a stalking fox rather than a well-disposed human, it could have snaffled the last two with ease as they sat waiting their turn.

On the water, they form another orderly queue heading downstream, all except the last one, which lags behind and suddenly thrashes the water to catch up. As it does so, there is a small flurry low down in the branches of an alder on the far bank, and the colour of that small flurry is kingfisher blue. Either the same two kingfishers that flew past me a minute before have doubled back, or two more have arrived from downstream while I was preoccupied with the goosanders.

They fly out over the river, where their reflections burst apart a patch of bright light, then they execute a tight turn round the alder and disappear behind it. Then another hour passes with glimpses of two young buzzards, some jays (heard but not seen), long-tailed tits and grey wagtails, a blur of dipper, but not a hint of kingfisher.

◎ ◎ ◎

Warm in the sunlit early afternoon, every leaf and blade of grass and flower a-glitter with the fruits of at least half a dozen hefty showers; when the sun shines, the land steams and the valley of this small Stirlingshire river looks briefly – and improbably – tropical. There are clouds of small birds in the alders, mostly warblers and long-tailed tits (the latter particularly prosper here). I have just settled into the lee of a small bank-side willow, where constant dripping on my head and neck is the price I must pay for shelter on such a day. Almost at once, the characteristic *"cheek-ee"* kingfisher flight call sounds close by. The bird apparently sees me only at the last moment, a moment when I wonder if it actually intends to perch in this very tree. But the flight deviates – only by inches – and instead passes a foot above the treetop, four feet above my head. The closest view of a kingfisher I have ever had reveals the neatly stowed undercarriage of bright scarlet feet tucked snugly into pale orange under-tail plumage. Every new view adds a detail to the sum of knowing, and with kingfishers, apparently no detail is less than extraordinary.

Minutes later, a small, bluish-and-pale-orange something-or-other whizzes busily on a dead-straight line between the island and a neighbouring tree from mine, one of those happenings enveloped in confusion by an intervening screen of foliage and an assumption that this bird is part of the essentially fragmentary phenomenon of kingfisher-watching in such a landscape. With my head still full of the kingfisher that just buzzed my tree, it takes a few moments more to realise what is going on, for the newcomer is suddenly clinging to the trunk, then it starts inching upwards, out of shadow and into sunlight, then it performs a vertical U-turn and descends the trunk head-first like an upside-down treecreeper. It is a nuthatch.

Three years ago, there were no nuthatches here. But thanks to a thriving population around the Scottish-English border, a tentative exploration of the south of Scotland has become a resolute northwards march as far as these fringes of the Highlands; a small, under-the-radar success story, nature as optimistic opportunist. I have been seeing them in very small numbers in winter flocks of tits and finches among the local oakwoods, but this is the first summer I have met them along this river.

Only now has it occurred to me that they wear hand-me-down, faded kingfisher clothes, and that when they fly low over the water there is more than a hint of the kingfisher-esque about their flight. But I imagine that only a mind so locked into the world of kingfishers as mine has been while on its mission to write this book would momentarily confuse the two. As soon as the confusion clears, I'm chuckling out loud, and the head-down-on-the-tree-trunk nuthatch raises its head and looks straight at the source of the sound with a "what's so funny?" stare, at which point the laughter gets louder. The nuthatch flickers away from the tree in search of tranquillity, or perhaps just saner company, a few trees further downstream, but as it does so, it arcs out low over the water, and it flies like a very pale blue kingfisher.

◉  ◉  ◉

The more often you go and the more thoughtfully you watch, the more you begin to detect rhythms or patterns that govern the life of whatever it is you are watching. It is true of all wildlife, all landscapes, all nature. Now, it proves its worth once more, for even as kingfishers begin to become truly familiar to me, so my presence becomes familiar to the kingfishers. In such circumstances, and if that presence is consistent and quiet and considerate and mostly still, there is every chance that they will come to think of it as a part of their landscape, and eventually ignore it.

By a process of trial and error over the first few visits, I have finally settled on two carefully chosen places to sit and watch. One is that little willow just across from the island, and the other is the original bend in the river a quarter of a mile downstream, where the views are expansive – not just a wide-angle swathe of river but also a broad sweep of floodplain with the mountain beyond. There is much more non-kingfisher wildlife here, and when a kingfisher does appear, mostly it draws "straight blue lines through bends and curves", in Henry Williamson's phrase (see Afterword).

Mostly, but not always. Here is a last-week-of-summer afternoon of rare benevolence. The river is high and wonderfully enlivened after the thunder-driven downpours of the night and the early morning.

Its voice is quite different. It is normally a conversational river: the audible sigh of the emergent burn and the twin midstream currents where the river takes the bend, the lowered voice by the far bank where the beaver dam's remnants slow the flow, the urgent edge where the small rocks reach out a fragmentary bulwark from the near bank... all these speak in their own tongues whenever the river level permits them to hold forth. But today is not like that. Today, the river travels with a deep, dark hush, with an aura of plenty and of contentment, all but overflowing with the last of the summer wine.

I have no way of knowing how these suddenly changed conditions also change the birds' relationship with the river (or the otters' relationship, the red squirrels', the roe deer's, the pine martens', the foxes', for they all must take the river into their reckoning every day of their lives), but its new mood has ensnared me in a remarkable way.

An hour ago now, I decided to sit facing the sun and the bend, and with the slightest turn of my head I see the mountain above the wide and tawny-grassed acres of the floodplain and the dark-green-forested foothills. The newly strengthened river binds the landscape together, and the landscape to me. For three days I have been deaved by a bug that made me sweat and shiver, denied me sleep and dulled my mood to something uncomfortably under the weather. And now, in the river's company, I can feel myself heal. It is as if the river has reached up to embrace my presence on the bank, as if it offers up an ambassa-dorial welcome on behalf of this landscape, which is as fond and familiar to me as any I know in the north of the world. I can feel my spirits lift, my body strengthen, and the warming evolution of a state of well-being. And out of that, expectancy arises as a skittish breeze out of a profound calm, and I warm to it as I warm to the resurrected sun, and two kingfishers fly past me going upstream, wingtip-to-wingtip into the sunlight. And if there is anything that outshines the magic of a kingfisher flying into sunlight, it's two kingfishers flying into sunlight wingtip-to-wingtip.

The bend itself is darkened by that thick wood-land from which the burn emerges. The water here appears to be a mysterious shade of ebony, relieved by vague and abstracted reflections of bank-side greenery, and by two parallel and rest-less tendrils of light where the sun has threaded the canopy in narrow beams. So the kingfishers fly towards the bend in what looks to the watcher like a sunlit trance, then in one transformative wing-beat they enter the realm of shadows and at once they become almost invisible.

Then, no less abruptly, they part. The bird nearer the inside of the bend – the far bank – takes the curving line of the river flat out and vanishes. But the other bird slows its flight, diverts across the throat of the bend, then rises to perch on a thin, overhanging branch just beyond the mouth of the burn. After a few minutes of preening, it flies down into the mouth of the burn, where a natural scaffolding of broken and leaning branches clut-ters the airspace just above the water, and there it perches, grows still, loiters with intent. In the binoculars it appears surprisingly dark, no longer a show-stopping head-turner, but a skulker in shadows, a spectre, a perfectly poised threat.

# FIVE

NOT TEN MILES SOUTH of that Highland Edge river, and halfway between a busy main road and the upper reaches of the River Forth, I have just stumbled into a Lowland waterworld of a thousand intimacies. Its every trait and gesture is at close quarters. A lazy burn (like most Lowland waters hereabouts) has worn its own trough deep into the soft, green underbelly of some of the best grassland in all Scotland.

My guess is that it takes a mile and a half to travel the 300 straight-line yards between the most inconspicuous of bridges under the main road and that point in the riverbank where the already mighty Forth swallows it whole without breaking stride. Somewhere in there, in those few acres of teeming and fairly recently planted young trees, head-high shrubs and jungly grasses, the burn has worn a groove so deep into the land that it has all but buried itself in fifty shades of green. You can see it from…well, from nowhere at all, and you might know it is there at all only because from time to time you can hear snatches of its mocking chuckle.

There is a way in, if you have the will to find it, and such a will is a prerequisite in the nature writer's toolbox. You will find it only if you consider that the brambles, nettles, hogweeds, willowherbs, flag irises, wild roses and other fankling species of vegetation designed specifically by nature to plug the gaps between trees and thwart your progress between the overworld and the subterranean banks…only if you consider outwitting these to be a price worth paying.

Suddenly the land stops. There is an edge, a short drop. Four feet below is a square yard of shingly mud, and you jump down hoping against hope that there is more shingle than mud in the landing area.

There are roe deer tracks, then otter tracks. And the burn appears to be flowing the wrong way. But because it doubles back on itself so often, a burn whose destination is north expends a lot of energy flowing south. The watercourse is narrow, mostly no more than two or three yards wide. The banks are tall and steep. And no casual passer-by would guess at its hidden presence in a hundred journeys. It must be one of Scotland's most unseen waters, which means its grey wagtails, warblers, sand martins, herons, roe deer, otters, water voles, fish – and its kingfishers – must be among Scotland's most unseen wildlife.

Deep within this submerged maze of looping water and almost islanded pockets of untrampled land, there is only one place I would call a space, "space" being a relative term in the circumstances. It appears at first glance to be nothing more than yet another tight little U-turn on the burn's erratic passage across the flat lands of the Upper Forth, but by one of the few stretches of navigable bank there is a swelling of underwater shingle, where the burn is shallow enough to wade across. It looks tempting for two reasons. One is because the far bank merges with a shingly slope that offers a dryshod way round the edge of a bed of massive reeds, and from the midst of which a sedge warbler is running through a more or less seamless, more or less endless account of its entire repertoire. You would not go so far as to call it music, but it is inventive and it makes you smile, and these are both good reasons to step close and listen. The other good reason to cross is that I have just caught a glimpse of a dancing alder tree.

Mostly, alder trees don't dance. Mostly, if they offer the illusion of movement at all, they appear to wade very slowly, the consequence of water levels rising (when they wade out from the bank) and falling (they wade ashore). But this one dances. Curiosity lures me across. From the shingle bank by the reed bed, it is at once clear that the burn's U-turn is much wider than it appears from the other bank, and at its heart it accommodates a deep pool. Right in the middle, the alder dances, its uncanny movements suggestive of a presence designed to direct water traffic. The illusion of dancing derives from two sources.

The first is the reflection of the trunk: the water is smooth but the current is strong, so the reflection ripples and creates movement suggesting a vertically held melodeon, and it vibrates the trunk so that the outermost branches tremble. The second is a broken branch that has not wholly severed from the tree, but rather it leans down at an angle and trails in the water, further enlivening the tree's capacity to dance.

A sand martin blurs past at somewhere around knee-height, then hurtles upwards to join a hunting pack a dozen strong above the crown of the alder. This is encouraging. Sand martin burns are often kingfisher burns too, and the lower branches of the dancing tree are perfect for kingfisher perching. Further encouragement: the silver sheen of a six-inch-long fish flips up from the surface, flattens out on the air and falls back into the water with a sideways splash. It's twice the size of anything a kingfisher could handle, but it offers my first confirmation of fish in the burn. Time to stake out the alder.

๏ ๏ ๏

It takes two hours, two hours during which the sedge warbler won't shut up for five consecutive minutes. After a while it becomes mildly irritating, then downright annoying, then the reverse happens and gradually the afternoon folds it away into hearing's middle distance, and it simply becomes a component in the soundtrack of the place, along with the voice of the burn and the wind in the willows.

Then: "*Cheeeek!*" The kingfisher enters stage right.

I still wonder if the alder's tendency to dance is responsible for what happens next. The bird rises from almost water-level to perch in the low branch that trails in the water. The branch that dances. The kingfisher does not grow still there, but rather it fidgets. I have never seen one fidget before. It constantly readjusts its grip as if it is unnerved by the movement coursing through the branch.

So why doesn't it choose a different branch?

No sooner have I formed the question than I regret it, for surely the kingfisher has perched there many times before and surely it remembers what happens when it perches there? But the branch proves to be not so much a perch as a stepping stone. The bird duly steps off and goes straight into a short, vertical climb with its beak pointing upwards at a shallow angle, wings working almost like a hummingbird's.

Six feet above the water it stops.

It tilts forward on the air, and now beak and tail are both pointing at the water and are held at right angles to each other, and thus the kingfisher hovers with its head rock-still, and thus the unpredictable movement of the dancing tree has been removed from the equation. Perched on thin air and looking down, the hunting kingfisher achieves a state of perfect control.

Somewhere deep in the confusing maze of kingfisher lore, there is a folk tale based on the bird's vanity as it admires the glorious colours of its own reflection. The truth is that whether on a

# KINGFISHER

low branch or in this head-down hovering pose, all
it sees of its own reflection is a small, brown bird
with a tiny, curved triangle of bright white at its
throat, like a neatly folded cravat.

# AFTERWORD

THE COMMON KINGFISHER (*Alcedo atthis*) is one of seven kingfisher sub-species. Its breeding range extends from northern Spain to the north of Scotland and south Scandinavia, and as far east as the Urals where it is a long-haul migrant, wintering as far south as north Africa. Otherwise it is mostly sedentary.

The British population is thought to be somewhere between 3,800 and 4,600 pairs, but Scotland has only around 450 pairs, a state of affairs that reflects a preference for the slow-running rivers, streams and canals of the south rather than Highland Scotland's mostly boisterous rivers and burns. It is by instinct a Lowlander, ranging between sea level and an altitude of around 700 feet. The kingfisher needs high, steep riverbanks of bare earth into which it can burrow a tunnel between two and three feet long with a nest chamber at the far end. It also needs overhanging branches or other perches for fishing, and lots of small fish.

In Scotland, the species is undergoing something of a renaissance. The *Book of British Birds*, published in 1969, noted that it was thought to breed only in the county of Renfrewshire, and attributed its sustained decline to water pollution and hard winters. Since then, we have made giant strides in the matter of cleaning up our waterways, and climate change has put hard winters into the "endangered species" category. The highest concentration of Scottish kingfishers is still in the south and south-west, but to one extent or another, it now graces most of the rivers and many of the burns of the Forth and Tay catchments, is gaining some ground on the Spey and the Findhorn, and has begun to explore the northern Highlands.

Young birds have an exciting tendency to go off-piste to unpredictable destinations when they disperse at the end of their first summer. Thus, from time to time, one has turned up after an open-sea voyage of several miles to delight visitors to the bird observatory on the Isle of May off the Fife coast. Others have startled birdwatchers in Orkney and Shetland.

Bizarrely enough, these sea-crossing episodes have an echo in the kingfisher's exalted place in Greek mythology. Halcyon was a mythical king-fisher believed to breed at sea. And while the eggs were being incubated, the sea would bask in serene calm and sailors knew they would be immune from storms.

The particularly striking blue of those tran-quil seas has attached itself to the colour of king-fisher plumage in the phrase "halcyon blue". And from the same source the English language has conferred on any sustained period of excep-tional good fortune the phrase "halcyon days". And Halcyon was Henry Williamson's choice of a name for the kingfisher in *Tarka the Otter.* In *Salar the Salmon*, the kingfisher is anonymous, but unerr-ingly portrayed:

# KINGFISHER

*...the kingfisher – smaller, faster, keener – drew his straight blue lines through bends and curves: flashing brilliance of emerald and sapphire changing to tawny underwing as it passed, narrowing blue again to shoot under the middle arch and pierce with silver lancing cry the stone-reflecting water-shadow.*

Literature is ambivalent at best when it comes to writing the kingfisher down. What you might call the "hail-to-thee-blithe-spirit tendency" is almost completely absent. That may be because kingfisher nests have an unfortunate, but not wholly undeserved reputation for indifferent hygiene, or it may be because of the bird's uncompromising way of rendering a small fish insensible before swallowing it whole. Either way, unstinting rhapsody is rare. The poet Norman MacCaig illustrates the point perfectly in a poem written in 1975 entitled "Kingfisher":

*...it vanishes into its burrow, resplendent*
*Samurai, returning home*
*to his stinking slum...*

Thus honouring a tendency for kingfisher burrows to reek of fishy slime and fish bones, presumably because housekeeping is beneath the status of splendid Samurais. And given that they routinely lay six or seven eggs and often have second broods, that's a substantial accumulation of fish detritus by the end of the summer.

Kingfisher nesting begins in late March or early April. The first conspicuous gesture of the nesting season may be the bonding ritual in which the male kingfisher presents a newly caught fish to the female. It is the only time you are likely to see a kingfisher hold a fish by the tail. The fish has to be swallowed head-first or the scales and fins would choke the swallower. A fish to be presented to the female must be handed over by the tail so that she can swallow it head-first.

The American poet Mary Oliver is a little more generous in her poem "The Kingfisher", but even here there is a degree of equivocation:

*The kingfisher rises out of the black wave*
*like a blue flower, in his beak*

*he carries a silver leaf. I think this is*
*the prettiest world – so long as you don't mind*
*a little dying, how could there be a day in your life*
*that doesn't have its splash of happiness?*

There are two fishing techniques. One is the
dive from a low perch (usually an overhanging
branch) above a suitable area of slow-running and
shallow water. The other, less often deployed, is a
hover-and-dive. Once the bird surfaces with a fish
in its bill and returns to a perch, the squeamish will
do well to avert their eyes, for the fish is despatched
by bashing its head in against the perch. It is not
pretty.

Adult birds usually stay on or close to nesting
waters all year, unless ice becomes a problem
in winter, in which case it will often head to the
nearest open water, usually a loch, a reservoir, or
the seashore.

Few birds are so addictive to watch. I have never
really got used to something so exotically garbed
and designed at work in my local rivers and burns,
never quite got used to the sorcery that imbues

its relationship with light and shadow. You have been warned. Once you succumb to the addiction, hours pass for the rewards which almost invariably only last for seconds. But you know you will come back, and back and back…

JIM CRUMLEY IS A NATURE WRITER, journalist, poet, and passionate advocate for our wildlife and wild places. He is the author of more than thirty books, and is a newspaper and magazine columnist and an occasional broadcaster on both BBC radio and television.

He has written companions to this volume on the barn owl, fox, swan, hare, badger, skylark and otter, and there are further ENCOUNTERS IN THE WILD titles planned. He has also written in depth on topics as diverse as beavers, eagles, wolves, whales, native woods, mountains, seasons and species reintroductions.

◉   ◉   ◉

Published by Saraband
Digital World Centre, 1 Lowry Plaza
The Quays, Salford, M50 3UB

*and*

Suite 202, 98 Woodlands Road
Glasgow, G3 6HB

www.saraband.net

ISBN: 9781912235032

Printed in the EU on sustainably sourced paper.
Cover illustration: © Carry Akroyd